My Cap of Darkness

My Cap of Darkness

Glover Davis

LITERARY PRESS
LAMAR UNIVERSITY

Copyright © 2016 Glover Davis
All Rights Reserved

ISBN: 978-1-942956-19-8
Library of Congress Control Number: 2016936029

Cover Painting:
Albert Bierstadt, "Storm in the Mountains," 1870

Book Design: Jill E. Crosby
Manufactured in the United States

Lamar University Literary Press
Beaumont, Texas

For Mariana

Poetry from Lamar University Literary Press

Bobby Aldridge, *An Affair of the Stilled Heart*
Michael Baldwin, *Lone Star Heart, Poems of a Life in Texas*
Charles Behlen, *Failing Heaven*
Alan Berecka, *With Our Baggage*
David Bowles, *Flower, Song, Dance: Aztec and Mayan Poetry*
Jerry Bradley, *Crownfeathers and Effigies*
Jerry Bradley and Ulf Kirchdorfer, editors, *The Great American Wise Ass Poetry Anthology*
Matthew Brennan, *One Life*
Paul Christensen, *The Jack of Diamonds is a Hard Card to Play*
Christopher Carmona, Rob Johnson, and Chuck Taylor, editors, *The Beatest State in the Union*
Chip Dameron, *Waiting for an Etcher*
William Virgil Davis, *The Bones Poems*
Jeffrey DeLotto, *Voices Writ in Sand*
Mimi Ferebee, *Wildfires and Atmospheric Memories*
Larry Griffin, *Cedar Plums*
Ken Hada, *Margaritas and Redfish*
Michelle Hartman, *Disenchanted and Disgruntled*
Michelle Hartman, *Irony and Irreverence*
Katherine Hoerth, *Goddess Wears Cowboy Boots*
Lynn Hoggard, *Motherland*
Gretchen Johnson, *A Trip Through Downer, Minnesota*
Ulf Kirchdorfer, *Chewing Green Leaves*
Laozi, *Daodejing*, tr. By David Breeden, Steven Schroeder, and Wally Swist
Janet McCann, *The Crone at the Casino*
Erin Murphy, *Ancilla*
Laurence Musgrove, *Local Bird*
Dave Oliphant, *The Pilgrimage, Selected Poems: 1962-2012*
Kornelijus Platelis, *Solitary Architectures*
Carol Coffee Reposa, *Underground Musicians*
Jan Seale, *The Parkinson Poems*
Steven Schroeder, *the moon, not the finger, pointing*
Carol Smallwood, *Water, Earth, Air, Fire, and Picket Fences*
Glen Sorestad *Hazards of Eden*
W.K. Stratton, *Ranchero Ford/ Dying in Red Dirt Country*
Wally Swist, *Invocation*
Jonas Zdanys (ed.), *Pushing the Envelope, Epistolary Poems*
Jonas Zdanys, *Red Stones*

Acknowledgements

I appreciate the editors of the following publications in which some of these poems first appeared.

Aspects of Robinson: Homage to Weldon Kees
Cutthroat
Miramar
San Antonio Express News
Solo Novo
Spillway
The Southwest Review

Other Books by Glover Davis

Bandaging Bread
August Fires
Legend
Separate Lives
Spring Drive

CONTENTS

- 13 My Cap of Darkness
- 15 Bear Song
- 16 Hyperostosis
- 17 Surgery
- 18 Dark Angel
- 19 After a Great Loss
- 20 Roses in Pots
- 21 Flight
- 23 Her Ruined Dress
- 24 My Late Wife's Clothes
- 25 Visiting Your Grave
- 26 Terminalia
- 27 Virtue
- 28 An Old Man in Sunlight
- 29 Pulsar
- 30 Dawn
- 31 A Scene Censored from the Seven Samurai
- 32 Sierra Foothills Autumn
- 33 C Dancing in Another Life
- 34 A Mare in the Night
- 35 Signet
- 36 Black Tower
- 39 The Magician
- 41 Retreat Into the Garden
- 43 Traveling Diebenkorn's Chabot Valley

44	Poppies
45	Wayne Tiebaud's Dark Desk
46	Wayne Tiebaud's Cakes
48	Mapping My Son's Trip
49	White Hands
51	The Mine Shaft
52	The Barber Shop
54	Fresno's Underground Gardens
56	American History
57	The Dance
58	Beneath the Mission Walls
59	Flying Home
60	Boulder Creek 1955
61	Revolt
62	At the Mouth of the Mississippi
63	The Quarters
65	Dulce et Utile
66	Song for Renewal
67	Earthquake/Mission San Miguel
68	A Small Town
69	Strange Maps
71	Trees
72	Rain After Drought
73	First Wild Flowers
74	The Corridor
75	First Spring in Texas
76	Mariana Reading Her Poems
77	Wild Music
78	Unfolding
79	The River Walk
80	The Neoteric Poets
81	White Herons
82	Pollard on the Road
83	Against Winter
84	Shadows

86 Aeneas' Dream
88 Silenus
90 Ambition
91 Above It All

My Cap of Darkness

1.
A photo in a yearbook catches me
as I lean nonchalantly on a green
bleacher, not posing, cradling a helmet,
paint streaked from collisions with running backs.
And I remember, how on several
occasions, the whole world went dark for me
as our heads butted with a crack, gold lights
twinkling on the black velvet of the sky.
For a moment, this helmet was a cap
of darkness without the capabilities
Perseus possessed, letting him move
unseen among various enemies.
If I could move invisibly among
those who discuss my life, my work
I would unsheathe a head whose serpentine locks hiss
and strike the air above my trembling hand
turning to stone the minds of those who think
they see my inner darknesses where gaps
of deprivation yawn, widening as they watch.

2.
Oh day of anger, when eyelids must fall
like curtains rippling down, and the vague spot
at the back of my skull, where a vein blew
apart, no longer buzzes when the low
pressures elicit thunderheads and bolts
riving the clouds with their white, jagged scars.
Then I will feel my cap of darkness pull
too tightly down, and I won't see or move

loose among the crowds on boulevards,
malls, parking lots—wherever my countrymen
would gather; and I'll know the time is near
when I won't hear spadefuls of dirt drum down
on a wood lid locked just above my head.

3.
Then sleep—until the day gold trumpets blare
hoping you will feel then, your bones recoat
with skin, and some fresh blood flow through your veins
somehow reconstituted, as loose dirt
drifts from your hair and shoulders, everything
suddenly bright, pure air in your new lungs.
Then rip your cap of darkness loose and stand
waiting with muscular ease for what must come.

Bear Song

James Welch and I were very drunk.
   He got down on all fours
chanting a Blackfoot brown bear song.
   Wind nudged the kitchen doors.

Dizzily we swayed on the rough tiles
   reddening beneath our knees
and did not see the moon's effects
   glowing through the banked trees.

We grunted, rolling our bleared eyes,
   glancing at our bare arms
as though a thick fur sprouted there
   invoked by magic charms:

bear teeth and claws threaded by chains,
   formations of firebirds
painted on Jim's sport shirt, the smoke
   of sweet grass mixed with words.

The family cat pushed through and stopped.
   His fur stood up like quills
and then he streaked through the back yard
   on grass where the moon spills

herself continuously through
   a bodice's ripped silk,
black against a bare white skin.
   Some spots seemed drenched with milk.

Hyperostosis

Bone spurs were forming up and down his spine.
He could no longer bend way down to pick
up litter in his yard or lace his shoes
or easily swivel his neck left or right.
His vertebrae were casing themselves in bone
as though his skeleton inherited
armor to ward off life's inevitable blows.

Some Celtic ancestors too often bore
the shock of battle-car collisions, axe
against helm, shield or leather casing thighs.
Somehow, over time, they printed in their genes
compensatory templates which became
a malady descendants must endure.
An x-ray photo shows a white haze spread
from bones around his neck and down his back.

Oh, let this man now move more fluidly
in his stiff cage of bones, remembering how
he once was agile as a dancing bear.
And let him have his cap of darkness so
he can move invisibly among all those
who thought he would be ineffectual
because of sorrow, age and this disease,
the gorgon which would paralyze him now.

Surgery

The surgeons whispering above would give
him a titanium and cobalt hip.
Perhaps the pain-muffling anesthesia let
some things rise from their unconscious sources.
But light from burning lamps seemed to congeal
into flocked gold—orchards, plowed fields, a horse
all carved into a cathedral door ajar,
trembling as though it might soon disappear.
He longed to rise, push through and talk to those
whose faces made vague lines against the light,
flowing through the bright jambs and on the side
where something like the wind half opened it.
He did not see the angel ether induced
when he was six and Doctor Warner cut
his tonsils out in a downtown office.
He saw this golden space whose entrance might
require his death and that which makes him live
would have to rise from his splayed body, left
seeking the splendor of a light-carved door.

Dark Angel

Drink from the cup of darkness she will raise
up to your unstained lips and let it ring
against your teeth the way fine china plate
will sound when tapped upon a bluet glaze.
Let the drunk bitterness purple and sting
your tongue, mouth, throat as folds of her ornate
brocade splash variegated lights across
your face, the stiff cloth crackling as she moves.

After a Great Loss

and after nights of absolute despair
he sinks into the cushions on his chair
and sleeps as dawn's light falls across his face.
Something in him loosens and his soul slips
into a white oblivion where it drifts
away from pangs of consciousness and lifts
and gently falls as though a hand had rocked
the stern of his small boat till he is shocked
awake by nuns when he was young; the glare
of a fluorescent light, his name, cold air
pouring through windows wrenched up near his head.
But in the day outside this room his dread
of loneliness may dissipate like words
chalked on the water or the air the birds
crisscross articulating joyous notes.
His particles of hope become like motes
caught swimming in an evanescent beam
fluttering on the white wall smooth as a seam
a scar tissue would make. But windows set
poorly are rattling as the curtains fret
and billow in a gust seething around
the loosened frames. Then slowly he will ground
his feet so he can rise to meet the day,
assembling thoughts, his clothes in disarray.

Roses in Pots

She put large pots of roses near our fence,
and now in early spring their colors blot—
white, salmon, yellow, red—on the intense
leaf-blades quivering beneath, each bloom a clot
unfurling on the waters of a pond.
Too often flowers this lovely seem to bear
some imperceptible edged thing a frond
conceals, petals whose piercing makes blood flare
from something like the thumb of a hand thrust
too deeply in a tremulous mass of green.
When the serrated leaves have filmed with dust
that's everywhere in summer, long stems lean
blown blossoms toward the parched, eviscerate
earth, showing forth this mortal beauty's fate.

Flight

Dead relatives assembling in the air
above her bed would talk to her and she
would answer them as though I were not there.
I could not see or hear any of them
but she would gently argue with Marla,
her sister, or with Leo, her father,
her mother, aunts, others I did not know.
I sat there silently and held her hand,
mottled by cancer spread everywhere
throughout her body, her pain held in check
by drops of morphine placed between her lips.
She couldn't speak at times or spoke in tongues
unintelligible to me, but there
were moments when her voice cut through the fog
of pain and drugs, rich, vibrant, generous.

Last week when I visited her I found
her drifting through her dreams and when I bent
to kiss her, calling her "my sleepy head"
she said "slept for weeks, so much weakness."
Later when she woke up she'd act out scenes
like a young girl. She'd pour some tea for dolls
or for her invisible relatives. For her
I was a man who lived in another world.
"Come back my love, come back" I did not say
the night her last breath rattled from her throat.
I sat there for a few moments then rose
and summoned nurses who checked for a pulse.
The breath the Holy Spirit gave to her
at birth had flown away like the huge hawk

she admired when it flew from its fence post perch as we drove down an empty country lane.

Her Ruined Dress

Our son sent me a photo of my late
wife taken just before her final course
of chemo whose chemicals would lacerate
her beauty once again, but in these terse
moments she smiles; some of her lustrous hair
has grown back, the pain flickering in her eyes
has become a candle sputtering for air.
Oh let time's regulating heartbeat freeze
on moments such as these before harsh scenes
etched in our memories by our own grief's pain
return again and we must watch morphine's
effects yellowing her skin with its pale stain
darkening day by day until the end
when her skin's a ruined dress nothing can mend.

My Late Wife's Clothes

There's a faint odor of her skin on bright
cloth she cut, stitched and wore against the sun
like primordial emblems of the beautiful.
If only a strong wind would fill these clothes
I'd stand out in the cold and once again
I would admire the gently curving hips,
and the black straps resting on shoulders where
my hands would light like falcons on a perch.
I'd cup them in both hands and gently pull
her toward me, lips lingering on fragrant skin.
I touch a sweater red as blood which I
once wrapped in tissue, placed beneath the tree
she decorated with strung tinsel, bulbs,
gold angels with our names engraved on wings.
I want to shut the door and leave this room;
do anything but bundle up her clothes.

Visiting Your Grave

Thinking you would have liked these roses' pale
orange colors I bring them to your gravestone,
cut stems in half and push them into cups
dug in the granite where your names and dates
have been incised with nothing else except
for a white cross entwined with a stone cloth.
It's hot today, and all around this place
the irrigated fields are sweltering.
There's no-one else here now, and I can talk
to you, my lovely wife, and only hear
in answer a hot wind up in the pines.
All this would soon revert to blowing sand
without piped water flowing into roots,
grass and white fountains foaming in this sun.
As you lay dying, you said I was lucky
but I bear your absence like a wound.
Someday, I'll lie forever down right here
next to you where my feet tread the dried grass.
In the distance, trucks gear down, moving toward
another desiccated valley town.

Terminalia

Oh God, we're animals bearing this gift
of tongues, thinking and dreaming, knowing more
than we should, bodies faltering year by year,
some new event erupting like a sore.

And though the syllables our mouths have shaped
could snare its essence with a perfect name
this act would temporarily end our powers
leaving the tribulation much the same.

And when the relevant discovery comes,
at last, it comes too late for most of us,
struggling through roughened currents which our lives
provide until we reach pale terminus.

Virtue

for Palmer Hall

"Leave it all on the field," our football coach
once said, our cleats clicking on the cement
locker room floor before we trotted out
onto a field chalk-lined beneath the ranked
floodlights where huge moths butted the hot spheres.
Tonight the field for Palmer is a room
reserved for readings, rows of folding chairs
packed with colleagues who seemed to focus all
their listening energies on this man's words,
his poems and essays as he stands and speaks
into a microphone, fighting the urge
to sway and tremble with his afflictions.
Such fortitude is what the Romans called
virtue, taking it from their word for man.
His right hand shaking just a little, he
stills it by an effort of his will and sounds
out syllables as though they are the notes
inked on a score which is his life tonight
and always; let us remember how he stands
bracing his voice against a malign wind.

An Old Man in Sunlight

Sitting in the sunlight, falling asleep,
he dreams of ink blots swirling on the blue.
Murders of crows go caw, caw as they sweep
down, black flags folding, some of them askew.
These semaphores have jolted him awake.
Rising, he curses them back into flight,
raucous complaints issuing from every beak.
Splashed syllables and feathers streak the white
air black, making it seem as though this were
just one more canvas of those things stretched
across his memory. So let him blur
in sleep whatever hurtful scenes have etched
their fluent lines as though a human brain
were copper, stone, paper with a flocked grain.

Pulsar

Now let what you have hurt
emit no piercing cry
like the exhausted bat
I crushed. And where he lay
on the white sill, as flat
as a t-shirt emblem
pressed onto cloth by an iron,
a stain shaped like a stem
leaked from his lips. No siren
summoned a blood-drunk host
from cellar, eave or cave.
He would dip, dart and coast
above, trying to save
himself from my broom, swung
over and over through
the air till his tongue hung
like a dog's tongue but blue
when he lit on the sill,
his impeccable radar
making him invincible
till then. But there's a pulsar
of agonizing cries,
to which this creature might
contribute as he dies,
pressed beneath his fright
and a book on the broom straw.

Dawn

A brightness creeps across the hollow, spreads
to the west through oaks and pines toward Chowchilla
lights.
They're dimming orange where coiled razor wire threads
the perimeter fences on the heights
above the women's prison. I once thought
spots glowing in the night might indicate
places where people rarely were distraught,
homicidal, drugged-up, drunk and where they'd wait
in pleasant resignation for a pulse
which finally flickers out on circuit boards
somewhere as fat-blocked arteries convulse
sick hearts letting mortality's curved swords
sever their breaths from life. But now dawn's rose
hues wash the sky near cells where prisoners doze.

A Scene Censored from the Seven Samurai

He rises from his reverie and cuts
a man in two so swiftly we see the halves
of his head fall before there's any blood.
The Samurai then meditates again
as though the death of the man challenging him,
then taunting him, never happened in a yard
sandy and bare except for one shade tree.
He sits the way the Japanese sit, legs
folded in front of him, a line of light
broken by branches wavering from his head,
to the chest of his patched robe down to his belt.
He's perfectly composed as though this death
is either meaningless or constitutes
the blossoming karma of a foolish man.
The serene detachment of this Samurai
startles me because I know I'd dream my hands
were smeared with blood and sticky on the hilts
of swords, on pommels, anything I touched.
But not this master swordsman who was taught
his own life's like a flower to be plucked,
admired then casually dropped onto the mire
trod by the hooves of squadrons passing by.

Sierra Foothills Autumn

We don't know how to dress because the winds
are volatile, changing from hot to cold
and back again as droplets on our skins
dampen our shirts until the white sleeves rolled
up make us shiver knowing we can look
for snow on distant peaks in a month or so.
Sometimes the seething leaves become a brook,
wind-borne and flowing towards a portico
so bleak even their final, brilliant hues
consuming energies cannot forestall
their dark extinguishing. If our skins bruise,
the swatches on branching arms, which sprawl
along a sofa's top, may seem like leaves,
struck places purpling under buttoned sleeves.

C Dancing in Another Life

with thanks to Peter Everwine's Aztec translations

Last night I dreamed you rose from "some deep flowers
trembling in bells and drums" and thought you were
the most exotic blossom I'd ever seen
if, as the Aztec poets thought, each life's
a bloom the sun brings forth. The orchids you
surpass have woven those diaphanous
fabrics which fluttered from your shoulders, gold
and glistening with their pearl-like drops of dew.
But one must usually wake to a world left
by those who've gone before whose patterns are
forever printed in our genes. Their lives
would somehow shade our own without the hues
the sun-bright petals drop around your feet.
But go on dancing to the flute and drum
shedding a cape of feathers, as orchids crush
beneath your sandals as your swaying brings
the circled Eagle Warriors to their feet.

A Mare in the Night

A mare's wet nostrils nudge me as I sleep.
Touch it and her smooth skin burns like phosphor.
Speak gently and she'll tentatively creep
onto the squeaking bed where a hoof tore
a coverlet the night before and spilled
me on the rug clutching a pillow stained
with tears, droplets of blood. I woke up chilled,
my night shirt ripped half off, my right wrist sprained.
But I remember silk against a thigh
and tender whisperings in a lamp's dim light.
I remember her lips parting on a sigh,
a woman like a horse with a sweat-bright
mane spreading damp on my blue pillow case.
A bridle slowly swayed with each embrace.

Signet

He dreams his polished buckles give his face the dewlaps
of a bull and add years and years to coppery features
of the minor Buddhas staring back above the straps
hooked, dangling, like slaughtered snakes the brass
immures.

When he awakes early or late and makes his way
to the kitchen coffee pot, he fills a cup.
Drinking the bitter potion he thinks he hears a spray
of roses tapping the panes till he looks up.

He only sees a brittle coat of rime, white as foam.
Leaving this room he'll search for any signet
not stamped but so lightly lingering on metal or glass any doubt
could make it evaporate like a drop of sweat.

Sunlight caught and dazzling lingers there.
Tiny illumined squares have made a honeycomb
on the frost-roughened glass before the banked cells flare
one last time and the melting sweetness of this light goes out.

Black Tower

1.
Leafing through magazines I came upon
a photo of a tower and studied it
from every angle, slowly turning it
beneath my pitted magnifying glass.
There wasn't much to see on those coarse stones.
Slick excrement and boiling oils had dried
and left a green patina on the stones
also blackened by sun, Greek Fire and smoke.
This happened year by year on a green mound
in Ireland not too far from pulsing waves,
shale-broken into foam along stark cliffs.
There are no gargoyles, no red dragons carved
in the thick blocks of stone; there are a few
dark recessed windows cut like slots way up.
But it was the roof where drowsy men at arms
would take their ease, letting their flesh absorb
pale light, heads propped against the battlements,
their helmets, jerseys, chain mail piled beside
them as fitfully they drifted into sleep.
But even then they'd check themselves before
they rolled into a crenel's open space,
and let some roving English archer draw
his long bow, piercing skulls, making them spurt
around his feathered shafts before he crept
away into the trees and underbrush.
One or two men might think the tower they built
with its encircling stones provided them
a cold incarceration, blocking out
most of the branches roughened by the wind

and the intense green glowing through the dusk
everywhere in the Irish countryside.

2.
A man at arms caught sleeping there once dreamed
the coat he wore, consisting of lapped stones,
made all the arrows or crude bullets glance
from his hurt ribs and granite cloth around
his knees repelled the tiny shrapnel blades
hissing through dust and smoke on the scorched air.
He felt his legs begin to petrify,
his arms' weight straining as they tried to rise
above his head, feet sunk in the soft earth.

3.
In Arthur Waite's Tarot deck there's a tower
struck by a jagged bolt with a huge crown
dislodged and plummeting to the toothed rocks.
Flames trail the king's red cloak like tattered cloth
as he falls headlong down outlined by tears
of gold and his queen's robe is a blue stream
gushing from a black window shaped like an eye.
A cone of fire erupts below one knee,
another on her shin. In a second, beams
of ragged steel protruding from the tower's
base, ripped halfway open like a tin can,
will impale her and knock her gold crown off.

Perhaps they should have substituted trees
letting innate seed forms cooperate
with rain and soil to raise leaved teguments
netting the blue, buffering the western winds,
attracting birds who would bring different seeds.

But out of fear and arrogance they built
a fortalice as gray, at first, as clouds
moving behind and through erected stones.
With smoke from fires, with natural decay,
with every mortal crime the structure shaped
like a huge "I" darkened above the land.

The Magician

The magician in Waite's tarot deck wears
a blue belt melting like the ice in spring.
Red roses just below have climbed some planks
and riot from bunched leaves in yellow light.

A horizontal figure eight floating above
his head symbolizes his own world joined
to the eternal-invisible whose powers
he would draw down, his right hand pointing there.

But now he darkens journal pages kept
for the first time, making a cursive flow
along the thin, blue lines where he describes
raw trivia spewed up on a sweltering day.

There he would pick through steaming piles to find
shards of glass saturating rocks below,
purple, red, green, the sunlight pouring through,
making some metals gleam like polished brass.

Oh, anything whose attributes might be
reflected in the words from which he'd build
poetic structures on the riven air.
Let his voice cut like a blade mottos engraved,

something magicians might raise against the moon
and stars, their symbols spread on trestled planks
in front of them, gold chalices, the sword,
black pentacles on disks, a budding staff.

He'd fashion dark similitudes on sheets
aflow with his inked images, desires
aborted stabs at meaning, ending somewhere
in the air or on a crumpled, littering page.

Retreat into the Garden

1.
Once at the San Diego zoo I stared
at a lioness; locked in her yellow gaze
I had to look away, walk quickly up
the hill from the lion's den, not sure that she
couldn't leap the barrier, though every sign
claimed this would be impossible.
I thought the world had grown so chaotic, roiled
by the events our newspapers describe,
it seemed to wait just like a pent up beast
behind steel bars or a deep moat with stone
sides polished to a thickness nothing grips.

2.
I'll walk into the back yard's deep green shade
with a card chair and sit propping a book
on a raised knee, reading as rustling leaves
soon register even the slightest breeze.
Some figs half-eaten by the birds or a green
fruit-beetle litter the cool earth beneath
the fig leaf canopy and smear the air
with an odor such as an unstoppered jug
gives off in a small room. "Try not to think
of anything or concentrate on just
one thing," as though in a deep pool the mind
has calmed at last and something may emerge
like a reflected blossom on a pond
whose slightest ripple makes the undulant
colors, the reds, the blues, the pale gold stripes

all run together just as the raw light
paints whatever the mind stretches and frames.

Traveling Diebenkorn's Chabot Valley

A light blue, roughly textured block may draw
your eye at first because it dominates
the canvas center where rectangles break
against its interrupted fields, dirt brown.
Perhaps these represent bare tracts, plowed up
and leveled just before trucks dump their loads
of gravel and their hot, black asphalt tides.
Blue could be an assertion of the grass
vital and spreading where development
would do its worst, but still black washed
the point of a triangle jammed between orange fields
and yellow fields bordered by darker blues
streaked brown resembling the polluted sky.
He climbed into the hills and gazing down
beheld another California valley
before bulldozer blades began to rip
away the poppy fields, knock down the trees.

Poppies

for Richard Diebenkorn

A glass of water on a table top
as gray as slate contains four poppy stems
and these erect their paper-thin orange cups.
Paint darkened at their centers makes two vague
shapes, one's something like a dove with spread wings,
the other looks like a broken hour glass.
Perimeters are lighter where it seems
the artist mixed more yellow in his paint.
A black floor frames the table with three stripes
vertically running down to the table's edge
but interrupted there. These stripes offset
a little to the canvas center's right.
I have no idea what these represent.
But the stripes may indicate Diebenkorn used
the golden section to compose this piece.
He has proportioned space so that a slight
imbalance may establish in the eye
of the beholder a residual sense
of movement pleasing to a restless mind
whose hot flaws turn it like a molten ball.
One glowing poppy breaks the white, red stripes
before they reach the slate the blue has touched.
There's no true stasis in anything alive.

Wayne Teibaud's Dark Desk

A roughened yellow line which must be light
has edged the desk's right side and made it seem
steep as a cliff. On an adjacent shelf
a porcelain vase holds apples on a cloth.
They're scarlet, but one shows white where teeth sunk.
And just above this, dark pools spill from the lips
of a cup knocked over. An address book's
light blue and aerial in any breeze
sweeping across the rich darkness of these planes.
A simple glass of water holds an orchid.
Its husk, bent over the translucent brim,
is light purple but its blossom seems so white
against the ink-dark and against its own
two yellow smears, it's ready to candesce
like an incendiary device and eat
the canvas with a spread of white-hot flames.

Wayne Tiebaud's Cakes

bear frostings red, tan, yellow, white or green
and the brush strokes are not more evident
than swirling textures bakers would have squeezed
from decorating tubes onto moist decks.
Another painting has depicted cakes
halved and their inner sections lined with dark
chocolate, but yellow as stucco in between.
I might slice through such decorated shapes
without regard for what Tiebaud has done
appropriating pleasure of taste to sight.

There was a huge sheet cake two of us slid
into the back of Lyle's old panel truck.
He had mixed food dyes with whipped cream, squirted them
onto a rough template of a bride and groom.
He printed letters, birds, bright numerals.
He stepped back sighing, cocked his head then made
some tiny changes and the whole two yards
of cake became a vivid-rough tableau.

Driving downhill we hit a bump and the cake
split as though a fissure from a quake
on a snow field decapitated bride
and groom and smudged red icing on a bird;
a line of text had broken from his beak.
I stared at the disaster right behind
us, as Lyle said "it'll be ok," and took
out his containers of whipped cream, his box
of implements, redrew the heads of bride

and groom, smoothed fissures with his spatula.

If Lyle saw Tiebaud's paintings he might say
"at least my cakes are real," and few could blame
this baker with all his practical skills.
But much of what we liked about Lyle's cakes
was their adornment, figures, colors, texts
demolished in a minute by our forks.

Mapping My Son's Trip

I trace your progress north and east on red-
lined encyclopedia maps. Today
you'll be in North Dakota, Minnesota
tomorrow Wisconsin and Michigan
then you'll be there. I put my thumb against
a red dot on an artery like those
someone once diagrammed on cellophane
in my old physiology textbook.
And there a portion of my heart will be
as long as you are there. (The Sierras mark
the eastern border of my real country.)
But I wish pressing my right wrist against
these paper lines would there transmit my pulse,
as though a map could be a poem whose lines
are often metered by a beating heart.

White Hands

for Chris

These moments which now seem so innocent
are marked forever in your book of life
where clouds of chalk dust make your palms so white
they almost glow in the late afternoon
shadows, which come in like a tide across
the desks, a book splayed open, a torn page.
Your blue parochial school uniform cords
were powdered just above your quadriceps.
You had to carry cardboard boxes full
of erasers out to the black top and bang
them together as you listened to the shouts
of children playing on a distant field.
You aimed a spit wad at the boy who shot
you first but Sister stood in the doorway
as you unleashed your rubber bands or else
she caught you passing notes to pretty girls.
Others could cover up and seem absorbed
by boring work on fractions or grammar
or catechism. But it was spring and fields
outside of Santa Barbara were rife
with wildflowers: poppies, goldenrod, lupine.
The breezes off the beaches beckoned you
as Sister droned on asking for a noun
or verb she'd scrawl in colored chalk where you
would run damp cloths when everyone had gone
into a languid afternoon not knowing
that this might be as close to paradise
as they would come for a long time. And years

from now you'll raise your whitened palms in front
of a mirror you dreamed and think these may
be emblems you repressed, though memory,
storing such things, insists they reappear
from time to time illuminating dreams.

The Mine Shaft

The shaft entrance gaped as though crossed planks
nailed there propped open a mouth where the teeth
were stones, carious, malodorous, slimed green
by moss and effluents from septic tanks.
And yet we boys would crawl between the boards
and move into the depths where earth and rock
half filled a tunnel one air shaft had lit
with a light hazed by particles of dust.
With voices clarion as trumpet notes
our fathers loomed above outlined against
blue mantlings of the sky and the sun's gold
radiance, eyes burning with their fear for us.
Tugging our ankles, wrenching some boards loose,
they pulled us out and we stood there ashamed.

The Barber Shop

Retired railroad men, carpenters with flattened thumbs,
brakemen, engineers and other workers
would gather in the barber shop on Higuera Street
and tell stories about the Depression, their jobs, the wars.
They'd welcome a young boy, let him listen,
show him the cardboard cutouts of the Panama Canal
being built, carefully placed in the front window.
Tiny men with wheel barrows, dynamite,
picks and shovels were placed near the raw dirt
which would someday be locks
flushed with water, floating ships.
The barber's father worked there, survived
malaria, came back thirty pounds lighter.
These old guys seemed gentle, wise, full
of wry laughter. Some had been Wobblies.
Some fought at the gates of lumber mills
in Northern California, Washington, Oregon.
All of them seemed to live somewhere near
the train station. One said he needed to hear
the engines in the night so he could sleep,
again reassured trains were moving
through his dreams up the Questa Grade,
down into valleys bunched with lettuces,
vineyards, orchards further to the east,
smudging horizon's wavering line.
If a train ran late most of these men
would pull out a pocket watch, tap
the glass case, sigh, and shake their heads.
The box cars clicking over the ties
became a constant pulse these men felt

in their memories, in their wrists and throats.
The boy would return,
if he could, but the barber shop is gone
and the old railroad workers
have long since gone into the earth.

Fresno's Underground Gardens

On Sundays men from C street strolled across
the baked dirt, hard pan running down five feet
beneath it, they would descend into the earth
down the steps Baldasare cut from stones.
They'd tug a bell rope and he'd scuttle down
a tunnel and appear unchaining gates
so these Italian laborers could work
with him awhile, then drink some wine, play cards
in a plaza still shaded by his trees
whose branches poked through a dome carved from rock
and shaped so that heat circled through the hole
where oranges, grapefruit, lemons dot the blue.
They worked in the San Joaquin Valley's heat
trenching for new gas lines or putting up
telephone poles they'd soaked in creosote
for days so that corrosive oils would coat
their gloves and burn the soft skin under eyes
when one or two of them forgot and wiped
away the sweat coursing in runnels down
their faces, chests and backs, blue work shirts damp.
Antonio Maggori, Joe Maduano
would rest in these cool depths, arms coiled like steel
wire braided cable when they reached across
the rock slab table for more bread and wine.
And you might see them ranged on either side
of Baldasare in black-white photos
superimposed on photos tacked up near
the entrance to this place where briefly he
presides like Pluton in this underworld.
Oh let these men return in the springtime

when the earth's fecund powers assert themselves
pushing all manner of living things through crusts
broken into the light and vivid air.

American History

Grandmother said some of our relatives
were handed rifles when they stepped ashore
at Ellis Island. They would assume new lives
in Union blue, marching into a war
they barely understood, their battle flags
emblazoned with a Vermont coat of arms.
Their new serge coats ripped into bloody rags
along rail fences on Virginia farms
so far from counties Cork or Roscommon.
Some of them struck by case shot, musketry
or bayonet would wade an Acheron
of blood, our civil war, but others thrived
awhile in places where we now may live.

The Dance

A feather's casual drift won't indicate
how birds with red splotched heads now underfoot
stiffen in the dust with piles of brittle leaves.
Teaspoons of blood matting their chests make coats
of arms shaped roughly like fierce animals--
a dragon or a sun-streaked eaglet's wing.
A pellet gun leaning against a wall
casts moving sun-dial shadows over them
till sunlight ebbs and silently an owl
glides down, its moonlit talons gripping one.
And wanton boys who did this thing now sit
before some burning logs which leave a mass
of radiant coals heating a cabin's one,
bare room against a first autumnal cold.
Woodpeckers pounding acorns in have pocked
the outer walls knocking and knocking all
day long until the fathers of the boys
gripped wooden stocks and with unerring aim
shot pellets into birds and laid them out
as though to fit them in a blackbird pie,
feed them to neighbors on a frosty night
when they pass jars of moonshine all around
then dance a victory dance knocking their heels
against oak boards not really knowing why.

Beneath the Mission Walls

I love the thick, adobe walls, the red
tile floors roughened by years of sandals, shoes
boots shuffling over them and the enclosed
courtyard where flowers planted in squares and circles
suggest an influence of Spain's Arab
architects who built in fluid stone
gorgeous geometries of eternity.
Year after year returning to this place
I dig through memory beneath these walls
as though my shambling presence bulked by age
could find some nourishing substance here where
my mother, aunts and uncles knelt beneath
a choir loft braced by large, rough-hewn beams.
I stand where Spanish archers must have stood
before they shot their bolts into the fur
of grizzlies digging for the sweet, white roots
which once grew just beneath the bank's black earth.

Flying Home

We're murmuring above the engine's drone,
leaning back, loosening our parachutes
in this B-26 on its last flight
to the graveyard for junked planes in Tucson.
When we arrive at noon there'll be acres
of fuselages way too bright in the sun.
There'll be B-29's, B-47's,
stacked rows of fighters waiting to be crushed.
Let a sculptor paint these metals and erect
some structures fierce and strange as ziggurats.
We take turns looking down through two portholes.
Beads of light threading the highways wink out
and the plains darken to the horizon
which lies somewhere beyond our throbbing wings.
But if the pilot caused the alarm to sound
we'd have to spill from the back compartment
into the wind, tug on our ripcords, hope
our nylon chutes would blossom over us.
Perhaps we'd land in a wheat field where waves
of grain ripple as far as you can see.
But that's unlikely. When we land I'll show
my furlough orders, catch another free
flight in an air force radar plane and land
in Sacramento not too far from home.
Our North America's recumbent now
as one by one we drift into our dreams.

Boulder Creek 1955

You could still see the pulsing steelhead fins
as the trout held themselves in place against
the currents, resting for their final push
upstream, deep into forests where they'd spawn.
They often lingered just below an old
stone bridge, pellucid in the deeper pools
as river waters polished stones and made
them seem like gold doubloons or bitten coins,
their silver heads and numbers worn away.
But now you cannot peer deep into pools
and, meditating for a minute, feel
pure liquid of your mind glide over stones.
There's a green scum from sewage and white foam.
Woven among the delicate reeds along
one bank are tissues, beer cans, plastic strips.
If there might be any residual powers
in this place, let them now assert themselves,
letting the river like a man despoiled
be just as angry, rise from clotted banks,
rip things from moorings tenuous with rot.

Revolt

If our oaks coughed the way sick men
    cough there'd be tiny dust
clouds where folds in the bark make lips
    and where sap forms a crust.

There'd be no syllables when stuck
    lips parted and no tongue
within to shape the sounds a tree
    might make unless wind-stung

branches lash and sing, some torn
    loose, littering the ground.
But let one oak lean forward, snap
    white rootlets all around,

step tentatively like a child
    learning how to walk,
its tall trunk tottering, a place
    for saws marked with blue chalk.

This might signal the trees' revolt
    against our ordinances
as the parched leaves articulate
    in flames their grievances.

At the Mouth of the Mississippi

Earl points to some bent trees, gray as old men
where the salt water has poisoned their roots.
Their shriveling lets the good marsh soil dissolve,
washed, God knows where, out into the Gulf where oil's
orange ooze makes dead zones, as big as a small state.
"Not long ago men grazed their cattle here.
I'd fill a sack with oysters and do it
quickly, get crawfish too and shrimp and eat
for a week or so on what I gathered here.
The goddamn Army Corps of Engineers
tried to control our big, muddy river.
The river's latent power could easily match
the force of all their thermonuclear bombs
ignited all at once. Those fools think they
can harness her with levees, change her course,
but sooner or later her sinuous tons
of water will shove aside the casements,
crush whole sections, sweep away the houses built
too low, even those raised on telephone
poles soaked in creosote or mounted on
huge concrete pillars slotted with rebar,
painted aquamarine or blue, some just
as gray as other things dying out here
along the southern edge of America."

The Quarters

We drive a graveled road deep into fields
where bladed, new canes ripple in a breeze.
And way out, set in stands of trees we come
upon the gray plank cabins, rows and rows
of them with their tin roofs and faded streaks
of green or white paint on north-facing walls.
We stop, take photos, wondering what it may've
been like when the slaves trudged back from the fields.
Sometimes at dusk, if you were near, you'd hear
their plaintive notes filling the air as house
by house their voices took up a refrain.
Imagine working under compulsion,
dawn to dusk, cutting cane in all that moist
Louisiana heat with mosquitoes
and other bugs flying up, sticking, skin
sliced by sharp leaves through tattered gloves or rags,
hands raw by afternoon, sweat stinging eyes,
men hired for the purpose urging you on
with subtle threats or brandishing of whips.
But knowing that your children would be bound
forever to a life as harsh as this
hurt some more deeply than the lash scars.
Escape? Perhaps, but this is too far south.
The land's crisscrossed with bayous, marshes, swamps
teeming with gators, water moccasins,
mosquitoes, leeches and the "patrollers"
who'd hunt you down with torches, guns and dogs.
But look, these cabins beaten by the wind
and rain from hurricanes still stand and rows
of them stretch back into shade-dappled groves.

Some of the slaves were trained in carpentry
and with their low grade lumber, hammers, hand-
saws, crude nails built these structures which would last
over a century—gray monuments
to sweat and pain, resisting servitude.

Dulce et Utile

Sitting at my desk leaning toward glass panes,
observing potted trees that never bloomed
before, rest lightly their exotic blooms
on the outer glass. These flatten like cheeks pressed
on dark italics lettering a store-front.
The petals are pale lavender with orange
circles and stamens jutting like poles brushed
red at the tips. How could the bees resist
such colors trembling in the first, cool breeze
bearing the first hints Autumn's on its way?
A blossom quivers when a straggling bee
alights on what may seem to it the source
of colors mixing odors in the wind.
Whatever it may be, something in me
too ranges out through orchards, gardens, fields
though I sit stock-still above ink-scrawled work sheets.
Let it return from every thought-touched place
with something "sweet and useful" for this page.

Song for Renewal

After four years of drought rain comes
at last ticking on the skylight,
washing the dusty, half dead oaks,
and the interminable blight.

Grasses on my hillside are gold.
Sluicing their dust the boulders gleam.
Because of this spring flowers may sprout
again beside our dried up stream.

Let water gently flow downstream,
the mule deer bend to drink once more
but moderate rain's turbulence,
all manner of living things restore.

Earthquake/Mission San Miguel

Saint Michael's cheek was creased, his breastplate split.
Some gorgeous blues had fallen on the floor,
their plaster sections powdering underfoot.
I dropped loose change in a red coffee can
half full of lustrous quarters, nickels, dimes,
washed by some candles flickering through the dark.
The sapphire at the center of his shield
parted as though a broad sword struck it there.
We had been taught Saint Michael's dazzling shield
could deflect almost anything but now
with painted armor pierced and his shield rent
he seems as helpless as a mortal man.
Oh let us now attend to Michael's wounds,
smooth them with trowels like a mother's hands
and brush blue pigment there so that our myth
of warrior angels may retain, in this place,
its visible presence, blue on white walls.

A Small Town

Because the air in this small Texas town
is soft and pure and leaves no grains of soot
on limestone blocks exposed a hundred years
or so, I think I could live here someday.
I'd spot an Air Stream trailer on a lot
not far from the town's center, stroll downtown,
drink coffee with old men my age who might
wear silver buckles won in rodeos
but tarnished now; they'd push back Stetsons creased,
sweat-dark along the brim, with scuffed up boots
beneath them as they murmur through the summer heat.
I'd compare this place to the red dotted towns
on California maps, their Spanish names:
San Luis Obispo, Mariposa, Fresno.
There'd be a man who'd raise his coffee cup
into a beam of light where I could see
an anchor stenciled on sun-darkened skin,
which webs a thumb to a bent finger—flukes
blue as sea water in those Mason Jars
holding dead specimens boys kept too long.
The tattoo's colors wash back into skin.
Mesquite, brown grasses rippling in the wind,
and the white sand out on the burning plains
blurred his eyes though dark glasses shielded them
as he rode down the strays he'd rope and brand.
Perhaps this speculation has its source
in movies or T.V. and then perhaps
no one in such a place would easily talk
to me or any stranger walking in.

Strange Maps

The buildings here are fashioned from limestone,
huge blocks carefully fitted with toolmarks.
The air has been refreshed by recent rains
and the sun's out sparkling breeze-shaken leaves.
So close your eyes and focus on one thing
and you will hear a plenitude of bird-
song coming from the San Fernando square.
But red buses drive slowly toward you and stop.
Colleagues, cousins, friends crowd their center aisles
or lean way out inviting you to join
them as they sing camp songs on their way now
to Pleasure Island or something like it.
When you ask where you are someone bends down
and whispers "Idaho" but you say "no,
this can't be true" yet you still ride with them
to a bus stop just outside of town and think
this is where I should get off and stumble down
into gravel as the bus winds uphill
cutting off most of what you see, a sky
so blue that gazing at it hurts your eyes
and ragged tree-top spears so green they seem
to glow with their own fire against the sun.
An inexpressible longing to be with them
steals over you like darkened cumuli
and you sigh thinking they have gone forever
into a block of color on a map
different from where you stand watching the bus
exhaust scrawl its gray font on the pure air.
They're moving to a state that should be named

Montana on a map you try to scan,
the wind fluttering it like a torn flag.

Trees

The pecan's leaves are yellowing in the sun's
pale, winter light, casting their flickering shapes
against the red brick patio below.
Two stories up I would observe these kind
of things through spotted glass above a desk
cluttered with bills and a page's blue black scrawls.
The wind shifts and through brightening glass the skin
on wrist and arm mottles as though some gray
flames briefly licked me there till currents changed.
No one comes walking down the street today
and there is nothing more to say except
the seething of the leaves, their ripping loose
resembles crumpled pages tossed aside.

Rain After Drought

Rain puddles all along our asphalt drive,
soaking the oak's parched roots, washing the dust
from trunks as gray as an elephant skin.
Wildflowers will sprout from the hard dirt, a lust
for water mollified, and purple-blues,
pinks, oranges dot these meadows once again.

If it were possible I'd try to stain
the air with vivid hues derived from words
or flaunt the kind of cape centurions wore,
red with a gold chain holding it in place
on a throat pulsing when cuts make blood pour.

But water turning into blood or wine
grows darker on lips trembling near a light
fluttering like a clogged heart shutting down.

First Wild Flowers

Wild flowers rise at last, poking green stubs
through wet-dark earth; new petals, tremulous
on the raw air, purple a porcelain tub's
white sides as I bend closer, curious
to see how colors can transfer their tints
the way a guilty hand not blood-drenched, still
can leave its whorling reds in fingerprints.
Scopes would illuminate a daffodil
of stains carelessly pressed on the tub's lip.
But it's the ground beside it where no seeds
sown by a human hand now sprouting, rip
through soft dirt into air, parting brown weeds
until each blossom opens to a bee
and pollen-drunk one lights on my bent knee.

The Corridor

The leafy north-south corridor outside
my window is a place where I will sit
on a card chair and daydream, read or nap
in the wind-shifting shade while roses drop
blown petals on my hair, my lap, my feet.
I'll touch the wooden fence with my left hand,
and leaning to my right the stucco wall.
My drowsy fingers will release my pen.
A breeze will bathe my temples and I'll wake,
my cheek bones slightly burned, my mind at rest.
And though the mind can be like a flaming mass
perturbed by everything, it now may cool,
its molten blossoms dropping towards the earth.

First Spring In Texas

Bluebonnets and Indian Paintbrush make
patches the breezes ripple orange and blue.
These motions cause the flowery mounds to quake
as though a lover's hands ranged over, through,
beneath a woman's hips, an upturned thigh.
Cruising curved roads where a light-shot haze gilds
the green, forget-me-nots reflect the sky
as variegated blossoms puddle fields.

Mariana Reading Her Poems

I see her on youtube and something seems
to melt within and it's not just her blonde
hair curling under, white lace blouse that shifts
a little as she turns her head, earrings
of green turquoise and delicately wrought
silver insignias flashing near her throat,
and not her voice touching the river plants,
or purple martins nesting in her yard
or even me watching her dance across
the hardwood kitchen floor, undinal hips
synchronous with the flooding harp chords plucked
from strings that resonate in every room.
No! It's all of these and something more.

Wild Music

For Mariana

We will return, my love, to this small town.
Where the Alsatian houses glow pale blue
or white with metal roofs which slope down toward
fenced-in plots crammed with vines, wild grasses, flowers
rioting against some weathered planks. There are
bluebonnets and red poppies cupping flames
in cell-phone photographs you took the day
I posed against the splotched, raw colors there.
I would have picked a red bouquet for you
but a dog lurking near waited for one
of us to touch his planks where blossoms scored
the wood like painted notes on blown parchment.
No Irish monk would emulate these staves
for any illuminated manuscript.
But loving their rough textures I would play
them, wondering what wild music I could spill
on the air and if they might give us a song
like a tune plucked from an Aeolian Harp,
wind in the strings, wind in your wheat-gold hair.

Unfolding

The pecan trees outside our window thrive.
Their new leaves sprout a lighter shade of green.
Thick trunks spread horizontally across
the yard, fifteen or twenty feet in length
and the squirrels come looking for pecans.
Racing across the branches they soon find
a few green nubbins here and there but turn
cheerfully away like farmers checking their crops.
They chitter at some dogs below. They know
that when the season's right these branches will
bestud themselves with nuts and they will eat.
Green masses mediate sunlight and wind
against the panes way up above the foot
of our bed, doing this as though impelled
by hands of guardian angels stationed there.
And we awake as children do at times,
peacefully meeting whatever the day
may offer as the feathering leaves dust glass.

The River Walk

A bank of lilies may reflect white scrolls
onto the river's marbled-green which rilled
by breezes rocks them in a wake, unrolls
their rippling parchments, letting the sun-chilled
runes briefly print vague capitals of light.
Such dazzling appearances might mean
nothing despite a fluency of white
dots, dashes foaming on the river's glassine
exterior, angelic texts which none
of us will read or ever comprehend.
And if eternity's graved colophon
crushes beneath a foot as leaves descend
one would still search the river bank to find
it trembling on the margins of the wind.

The Neoteric Poets

When power-drunk generals decided things
they massed their cohorts in a city square.
Anyone trying to stop them could be "proscribed."
You'd see his head impaled on an iron spike,
and this is how they murdered Cicero.
The Republic died forever on that day.

The unnamed Emperor might take his seat
with other senators but they all knew
wherever he might sit would be a throne.
Because of this the Neoteric Poets
retreated to their gardens; there would be
few patriotic poems, no epics till
Virgil composed the Aeneid despite
himself but instructed his heirs to burn
it when he died.
                      Virgil, Propertius,
Horace and Catullus all believed they should
concentrate on details: "keep your sheep fat
and your lines thin."
                          We are so much like them,
carding our lives for things we'd weave like wool
into the lines we station on a page.
Disgusted by our governments, puerile and corrupt,
we will concern ourselves with little things
surrounding us in the green shadows, moist
from watering like the blossoms just beyond us
in patches of light swaying on their stems.

White Herons

The river's paved walks wind along its banks
above the water rippling green where trees
reflect a stippling of branches and trunks.
A water gate retards three floating planks
and sinks beneath them as twin launches squeeze
through, wobbling for a moment like two drunks.
All of the white herons have flown away,
though drought has not diminished the cool springs
erupting from the earth, feeding this stream.
But let me pluck some plumes pearled by the spray
from a boat's wake, let wind fan them like wings,
candescent, in these hands, raised once, in a dream.

Pollard on the Road

As Pollard moves into the wind his hair
parts briefly, white as blossoms or the snow
he's rarely seen. It flurries through the air.
Something has broken from him like a floe,
blue-edged and bitter drifting from its source.
The day before Pollard watched from his plane
as clouds beside him shaped a Trojan horse
with melting winds. But soon a blinding rain
erased it and two rows of running lights
like feathers on a shaft helped guide to earth
his jumbo jet. Lately Pollard alights
in a recurring dream of death or birth
from something similar; its painted wheels
pock the asphalt as reddened pools and bands
of shivering lights reflect onto his coat,
illuminate his hands and face, his cap
of burning hair. Out where large bodies float
or thump onto the tarmac, where jets snap
through flame or thunder, wings lit green or blue,
Pollard could be a modern Mercury.
But all his messages garble, pouring through
fingers raised to shield a bloodshot eye.
A brightening motel room wakes Pollard up
and once again he's what he's come to be.
Rubbing his eye dissolves his melting cup
of dreams and he must face a mundane life
in a northern city, dressed in a wool suit.
Outside beneath some trees a fluttering leaf
tears loose from its gray stem, some distant roots.

Against Winter

Black heads with red splotches whir up
and down, beaks tapping through the day
like tiny hammers pocking walls,
some window sashes, a doorway.

Some acorns jammed into the sides
fell when we wrenched open a door,
plywood on hinges rusted shut.
This seemed like tape ripped from a sore.

A rubber spider dangling black,
big as a fist with filaments
for hair, jouncing in a west wind
raking the eaves, may loom immense

in a black bird's eye as it sweeps down—
repulsed, wings braking in mid-air.
But woodpeckers ignore such things,
making the red of their heads flare.

There's nothing we can do to stop
them, nothing frightens them for long.
Chase them away and they will soon
return with a wood-tearing song.

Shadows

I once admonished ravens who had ripped
the screens from my front windows, their black plumes
whipping the glass, beaks hammering because
they'd eaten dog food spilled on my front deck
and wanted more. When I cursed them, they flew
into the pines as though they understood
how human words might somehow wound, not quite
like birdshot soon to follow if they stayed.

This raven's raindrop-speckled wings unfurled
and he took flight from our drenched eaves,
seeming to leave a shadow on the wall
beneath the panes through which he had peered down.
He may have thought we were like animals
immured in the pit of rooms we'd never leave,
while he felt buoyant currents under him,
helping him glide for miles across the blue.

The shadow moving down the wall has rough
cut wings, a flattened beak, though it could be
whatever any one of us might need
to see flickering where a glowing log
casts its firelight, then crashes on screened bricks.
Tomorrow I might think it's just a stain
caused by a ruptured pipe or cracked roof tile.

The raven may have warned me in a dream
I can't remember very well--a swatch
of feathers gray and shifting on the wall
like some leaf-shadows dancing just before

a north wind rips them from their stems and they
come down the way each one of us might fall
on that bleak day assigned to us, our breaths
rattling from our throats, beating pulses stopped.

Aeneas' Dream

Translation from Virgil

Hector appeared before me in a dream.
But as he tried to speak his huge tears poured
from pain-filmed eyes. Because Achilles dragged
him from his chariot there was a dark
 and bloody dust on thong-pierced swollen feet.
Alas, this Hector had so greatly changed
from he who put on the spoils of Achilles
stripped from Patroclus then gave them back,
from the man who led the Phyrgians with pitch-
soaked torches on the decks of the Greek ships.
Wearing a filthy beard matted with blood
he took more wounds around his country's walls.
Weeping further I, myself, seemed to speak
to this hurt ghost and brought forth these sad words:
Oh most faithful of the Teucrians,
Oh light of the Dardanians, what great
hindrance kept you from those who eagerly
waited to see you coming from the shore?
Though we are worn out by the many deaths
of our soldiers and by the various
labors of our men and city, how gladly we
see you again, but what undeserved cause
has marred the fair expressions of your face,
and why am I now seeing all these wounds?
He said nothing, nor was my asking him
a useless hindrance, nor did he heed me
as I sought useless things, but finally
forming a groan deep in his chest he said,

"Alas flee, child of the goddess, rescue
yourself from all these flames. The enemy
has taken our high walls. Troy rushes down
from its great pinnacles into the depths.
You gave enough to Priam's country.
If I could have defended Pergama
with this right hand, it still would be protected.
Troy entrusts to you its sacred things,
its household gods, so take these comrades fate
bestowed on you. And seek with them the great wall
you finally will establish after you have
wandered over the turbulent seas."
He lifted from a shrine a vestal god,
powerful and eternal, and with his hands
brought forth garlands, cupping in his palms
their glowing, inmost, perpetual flames.

Silenus

Old people often claimed a man
back in the hills could play
a flute or a guitar so well
all the tree tops would sway

in rhythm with his metered notes
which vivified the power
residing in oaks, meadows, brooks
and helped the fruit spurs flower.

If somehow you could corner him
reclining on a swing,
leaf-mottled on a white-washed porch
then make the fat man sing.

But be alert, for he might try
to lull you with a song
so lyrical that when he tried
to vault the rail along

the porch side strewn with fallen leaves
you might not see him merge
with shadows pooling where cool winds
whisper as they emerge.

You'd like to find goat hooves beneath
his cuffs, and tiny horns
below curls plastered to a brow
no ivy wreath adorns.

You'd only have a man whose paunch
will jiggle when he moves,
whose hair is ash, but let him chant
and much of this dissolves.

Rapt from the moment by his notes
white-candid and so pure
you could almost believe what myths
have said about the power

a poet once possessed to make
the tree tops nod their heads
and flaming groves descend hillsides,
light-drunk as gray dusk spreads.

Ambition

Drive through our great southwestern deserts, gaze
upon the massive ridges, purple-gray,
when the light changes under shifting clouds
and wonder if a man could somehow share
these attributes if a mind expands the way
we have been told it might or sometimes has.

Let wind drive clouds into a mountain peak,
rip the gauzed vapors like a tattered cloak.
Let this reveal escarpments blue with ice
and where the melting sun breaks through, huge slabs
of granite, blue-gray, tan or rust veined, gleam
like the oiled muscles lifters often pump
in front of mirrors with chalk-dusted hands.

There is a perfect stillness mountains may
achieve when the tectonic plates don't shift,
no gases seep into the air, no red
eruptions spew their flowing magmas down,
igniting trees and flowers, luckless cars,
each mountain rolling like an elephant.
Let each one sink onto its own broad base,
compose itself, and its imperial calm
will dominate the countryside for miles
and miles until the cumuli shroud it.

Above It All

Mists rise from my front meadow where the oak
branches obscure whatever lies far down
these hills in the flat valley where the truck
lights blurring spread their cotton on the air.
Whirring down ninety nine like freight trains run
off broken tracks they suddenly appear
as ghost trains, sometimes ramming slower cars.
You can hear whirlwinds their power generates
before they pass you like something right out
of hell, these burnished battle cars with scythes,
death heads, doors pin-striped with confederate flags.
So I'll stay home until the sun burns through
and perched like an eagle up above it all
in my hilltop home where the air remains
pure and I can look down for miles and miles.
When the sun comes out at last the lit cars flare
and disappear as they race towards the coast.
But from my vantage point I nod above
my yellow legal pads and clouds of sleep
puff from my mind as I try to wield my pen.

I think of the Iliad and Mitchell's new
translation where the Seasons gently strip
gold bridles from White Horses of the sun,
feeding and stabling them near Mount Ida
as Lord Zeus reclines upon a cloud,
ignoring blood-choked mouths, death-dusted eyes
and corpses piled up near the Scaaen Gates.
Though he naps now, he previously took
pleasure from mingling, sometimes disguised, sometimes

invisible, with mortals who must die
"clattering to earth in gleaming armor"—brains
chests, livers pierced with arrows, blades, spear-points.
He loved to toy with them, favoring one side
and then the other as the battle moiled
across the beaches close to the black ships.
And all the lesser gods were even more
mischievous, like Hera who would beg
Aphrodite to help her seduce Zeus,
distracting him when Hector needed help,
and Poseidon, who rose from the sea to shake
the earth and aid his faltering Argives.

And even now do similar powers sweep
over and around us, invisible
as the winds driving blue Pacific swells?
Could they determine human destinies,
altering our passages through time and space?
Homer would think so. I don't want to know.
And though I have observed things from these heights,
when the right time comes I'll move into a world
below where things can be touched, tasted, heard
and try to be as solid as a house,
strong as a horse, white blazings on the throat—
at least in vivid dream-fueled reveries—
but finally only a mortal, aging man.